Practise and Pass

Cambridge Young Learners English Test

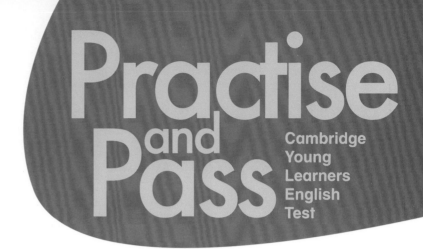

MOVERS

Pupil's Book

GW00728812

Cheryl Pelteret and Viv Lambert

DELTA Publishing
Quince Cottage
Hoe Lane
Peaslake
Surrey GU5 9SW
United Kingdom
www.deltapublishing.co.uk

First published 2010

Project managed by Chris Hartley
Edited by Barbara MacKay
Designed by Peter Bushell
Illustrations by Claire Mumford, Geo Parkin and Peter Stevenson
Printed by: Melita Press, Malta

ISBN: 978-1-905085-39-2

Contents

Listening PART **1**

Step 1 – Prepare

1 Listen and number the pictures. 🎧 1

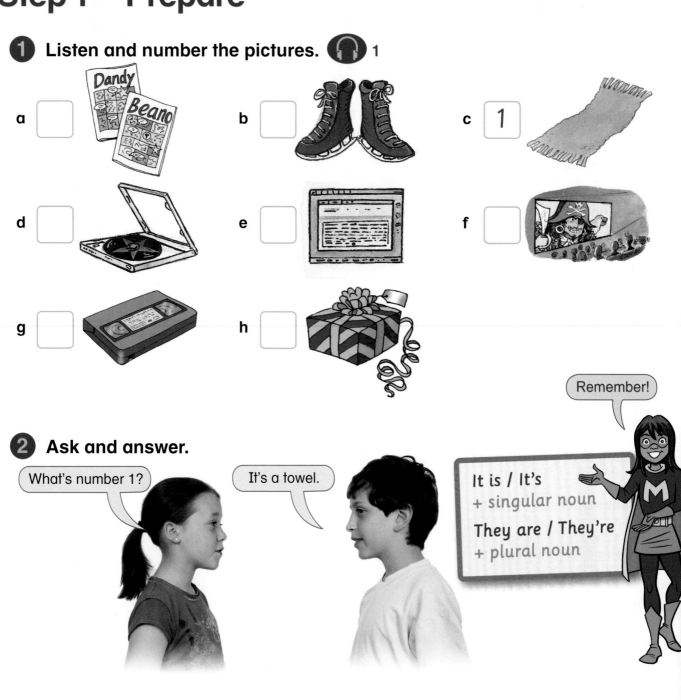

a [ ]   b [ ]   c [1]

d [ ]   e [ ]   f [ ]

g [ ]   h [ ]

Remember!

It is / It's
+ singular noun

They are / They're
+ plural noun

2 Ask and answer.

What's number 1?

It's a towel.

3 Find and write the words from exercise 1.

1 .....towel.....   5 ....

2 ....   6 ....

3 ....   7 ....

4 ....   8 ....

d	v	c	a	t	a	l	c
v	i	d	e	o	p	e	o
p	o	s	a	w	p	d	m
p	a	k	r	e	w	o	i
e	m	a	i	l	e	n	c
e	a	t	v	i	d	y	s
p	r	e	s	e	n	t	r
r	o	s	f	i	l	m	t

4 Write the words.

1 m i n g m i w s   l o p o
swimming pool

2 V D D   p r e y a l
....

3 t a s g k i n
....

4 e m a n i c
....

5 p t a y r
....

6 D C   l a p r e y
....

5 Match. Write the words from exercise 4.

1 Daisy's the girl who's got a towel.

2 John is the boy who likes watching films.

3 Fred and Jane are carrying presents.

4 Sally's the girl who's got some skates.

5 Jim's the boy who's got a CD.

6 Mary is watching a DVD.

a She is good at ....

b It's their friend's ....

c She's using the ....

d When it's hot, she goes to the _swimming pool_ .

e He's listening to a CD on the ....

f He wants to watch a film at the ....

6 Ask and answer.

Who's Daisy?

She's the girl who's got a towel.

Remember!

who + is = **who's**

who + has = **who's**

Step 2 – Practise

1 Listen and write the names. 🎧 2

1 _Daisy_   2 ....   3 ....   4 ....   5 ....   6 ....

2 Listen and draw lines. 🎧 3

1 Jill
2 Alex's dad
3 Kim and Lucy
4 Alex
5 Ben
6 Bill

a

b

Remember!
Draw clear lines.

c

d

e

f

Step 3 – Pass!

1 Listen and draw lines. There is one example. 🎧 4

Vicky   Daisy   Sally

Fred   Peter   John

Step 1 – Prepare

1 Write the six places.

1 You go swimming at a **swimming p** ool
2 You can do sports at the **sports c** ....
3 You can read books here. **l** ....
4 You can have a drink or a sandwich here. **c** ....
5 You can buy food, drink and clothes here. **s** ....
6 You can watch a film here. **c** ....

2 Write the words. Listen and check. 🎧 5

1 swimming pool   2 ....   3 ....

4 ....   5 ....   6 ....

3 Look and write the words.

1 She had a .... cup .... of coffee at the café.
2 They saw a .... the cinema
3 She .... in the swimming pool.
4 She went .... at the supermarket.
5 She read a .... at the library.
6 They played .... at the sports centre.

| book |
| ~~cup~~ |
| film |
| shopping |
| swam |
| table tennis |

4 Look and draw a line to match the words and pictures.

1 farm
2 hospital
3 market
4 bank
5 road
6 bus station

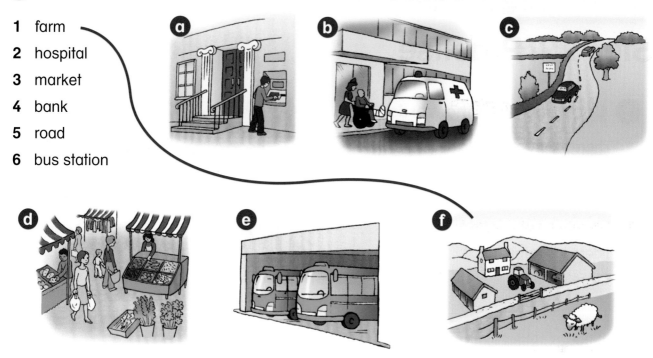

5 Look and draw a line to match the questions and the answers.

1 Where did you go?   We took a bus from the bus station.
2 When did you go?   My friend, Paul.
3 How did you get there?   A cup with an animal on it!
4 Why did you go?   To a farm.
5 Who did you go with?   On Tuesday.
6 What did you buy?   To see the animals.

6 Look and write.

M o n day

T _ _ _ day

_ _ _ _ _ _ sday

T _ _ _ _ _ day

F _ _ day

_ _ _ t _ _ day

S _ _ _ day

Remember!

Monday, not monday

9

Step 2 – Practise

1 **Look and write the words.**

1 There's a **kanb**. _bank_
2 There's a **ketmar**. ....
3 There's a **rybrail**. ....
4 There's a **sub niotast**. ....
5 There's a **talpisho**. ....
6 There's a **dora**. ....

2 **Ask and answer.**

How do you spell 'bank'?

B-A-N-K

3 **Listen and circle the words.** 🎧 6

When: (Wednesday) / Monday
1 Where: to the beach / to the sports centre
2 How many children: 12 / 16
3 Travel: by bus / by car
4 Weather: windy and cold / warm and sunny
5 Favourite activity: swimming / skating

Step 3 – Pass!

 Listen and write. There is one example. 7

The farm

When: Saturday ....

1 Where: ....

2 Who: ....

3 How: ....

4 Bought: ....

5 Favourite thing: ....

Step 1 – Prepare

1 **Look and draw lines.**

| bus station | ticket | driver | motorbike | lorry | bus |

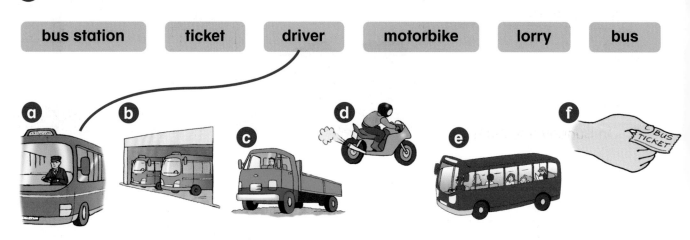

2 **Look and write the words.**

buy catch ~~drives~~
fly ride sail

1 My dad _drives_ a car.

2 You can .... the bus outside the bus station.

3 We .... across the sea on a boat.

4 We .... to Australia in a plane.

5 Does your dad .... a motorbike?

6 You .... a ticket at the station.

drive + car, bus, lorry
ride + bike, horse, motorbike

Remember!

3 **Listen and draw lines.** 🎧 8

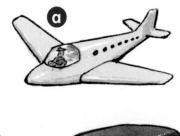
driving a car

sailing a boat

flying a plane

buying a ticket

4 Write the past tense verbs. Do the crossword.

Across

3 We ...played... tennis on Saturday.

4 After the game, we .... TV.

6 In the evening, I .... to my friend's house by bus.

Down

1 We .... in the park on Saturday. I love skating.

2 On Sunday, my mum .... a cake.

4 I .... to the park.

5 My friend .... with me to the park.

6 It .... a good day!

5 Look and write about the weather.

1 On Monday, it _was cold_ .

2 On Tuesday, it ....

3 On Wednesday, it ....

4 On Thursday, it ....

5 On Friday, it ....

6 On Saturday, it ....

7 On Sunday, it ....

Listening PART 3

Step 2 – Practise

1 Listen. Write *T* (true) or *F* (false). 9

1   On Monday Jenny had a picnic with her friends.   ...T...
2   It was warm and sunny on Tuesday.   ....
3   On Wednesday she skated, because it was windy.   ....
4   She went shopping on Thursday.   ....
5   On Friday she stayed at home.   ....
6   On Saturday the children had lunch in the cafe.   ....

2 Listen again and draw lines. 10

Monday

Tuesday

Wednesday

Thursday

Friday

Saturday

Sunday

3 Ask and answer.

When did Jenny go on a trip?

On Tuesday.

14

Step 3 – Pass!

1 What did Jane do last week?
Listen and draw a line from the day to the correct picture. 11
There is one example.

Monday

Tuesday

Wednesday

Thursday

Friday

Saturday

Sunday

Listening PART 4

Step 1 – Prepare

1 Write the food and drink words.

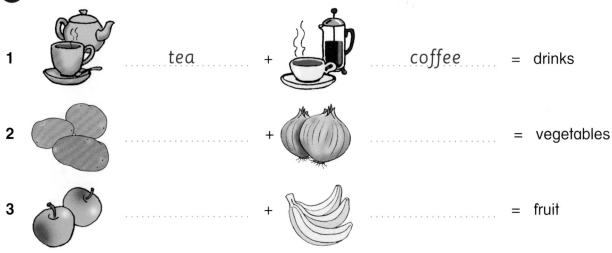

1 ....tea........... + ...coffee.......... = drinks

2 .... + ... = vegetables

3 .... + ... = fruit

2 Write the words in the correct box.

grapes   ~~lemonade~~   watermelon   pineapple   water   carrots

Drinks
lemonade

Fruit

Vegetables

3 Ask and answer.

What's your favourite food?

Fish and chips!

④ Find and write six food and drink words.

w	g	e	g	v	t	h	a	y	u
f	y	c	h	e	e	s	e	h	s
j	l	o	r	g	a	o	l	l	n
c	m	f	a	e	r	u	t	q	o
t	z	f	s	t	a	p	p	m	x
p	n	e	p	a	s	t	a	u	i
s	b	e	b	b	l	e	r	z	b
k	w	s	a	l	a	d	t	c	d
a	o	e	g	e	s	l	p	u	r

1 cheese
2 ....
3 ....
4 ....
5 ....
6 ....

⑤ Write the words.

cup	bottle	bowl	glass

1 a ....glass.... of water

2 a .... of coffee

3 a .... of soup

4 a .... of salad

5 a .... of lemonade

6 a .... of orange juice

⑥ Listen and write. 🎧 12

1 Mum wants to have a   bowl   of   soup   .

2 Dad wants to have a .... of ....

3 Vicky wants to have a .... of ....

4 Alex wants to have a .... of ....

Remember!

I want a
cup of tea.

Step 2 – Practise

1 Listen and tick ✔ the box. 🎧 13

1

2

3

2 Listen again. Put a tick ✔ or a cross ✖ in the box. 🎧 14

1 It was sunny on Saturday. ✔

2 Five children went for a picnic.

3 Bill brought all the drinks and food.

4 All the children like lemonade.

5 Lucy brought some chocolate cake.

6 Sue didn't bring the sandwiches.

Listen to the whole dialogue, then answer!

Step 3 – Pass!

1 Listen and tick ✔ the box. There is one example. 🎧 15

1 Where did Ann go on Friday?

A  ✔

B

C

2 What does she want to make for her party?

A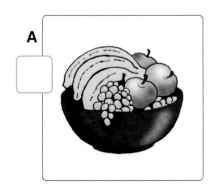

B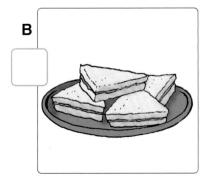

C

3 What didn't she buy?

A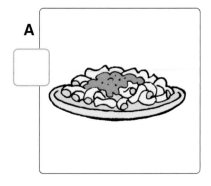

B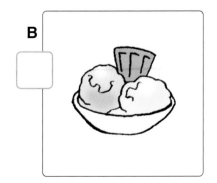

C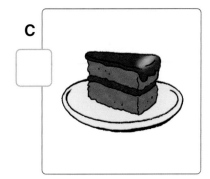

Listening PART **5**

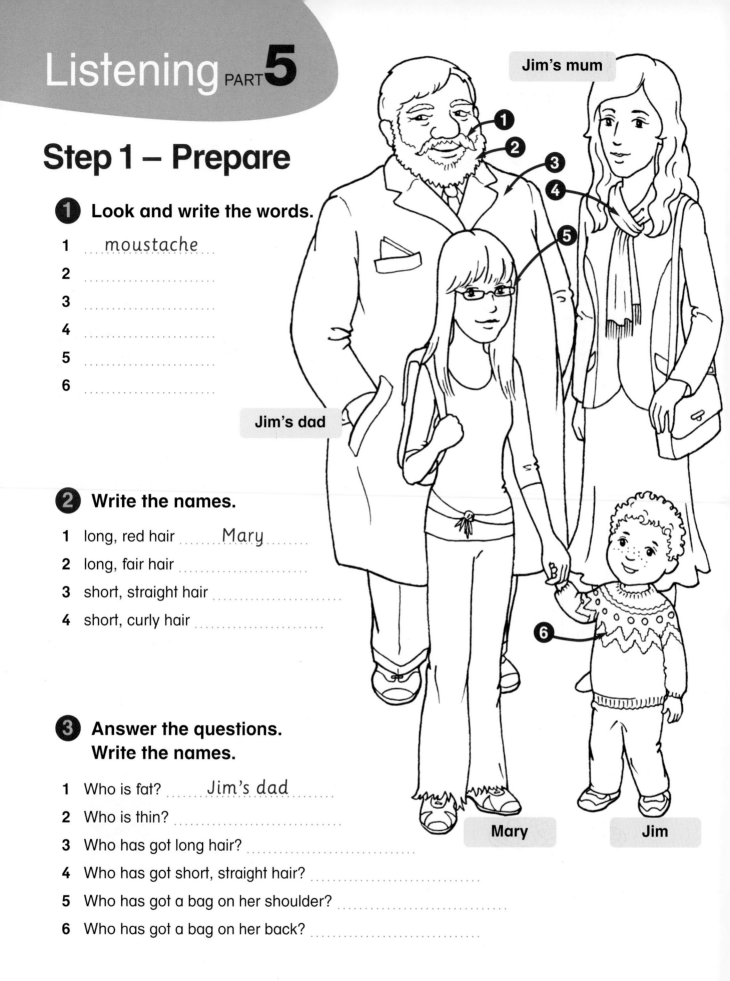

Jim's mum

Jim's dad

Mary

Jim

Step 1 – Prepare

1 Look and write the words.

1 _moustache_
2 ....
3 ....
4 ....
5 ....
6 ....

2 Write the names.

1 long, red hair ...._Mary_........
2 long, fair hair ....
3 short, straight hair ....
4 short, curly hair ....

3 Answer the questions.
Write the names.

1 Who is fat? ...._Jim's dad_........
2 Who is thin? ....
3 Who has got long hair? ....
4 Who has got short, straight hair? ....
5 Who has got a bag on her shoulder? ....
6 Who has got a bag on her back? ....

4 Listen and colour. 16

5 Write the words.

above	~~next to~~	below	near	inside	opposite

1 A boy is standing .... **next to** .... a girl.

2 They are .... the cinema.

3 A woman is .... the boy and the girl.

4 The boy and the girl are standing .... the man.

5 There's a fan .... the man's desk.

6 There's a bag .... the desk.

6 Write *T* (true) or *F* (false).

1 The boy is wearing a sweater.   ....F....

2 The girl is wearing a scarf.   ....

3 The boy is wearing a coat.   ....

4 The man hasn't got a beard.   ....

5 The man has got long hair.   ....

6 The girl has got short, curly hair.   ....

7 Listen and colour. Ask and answer.   17

What colour is the boy's scarf?

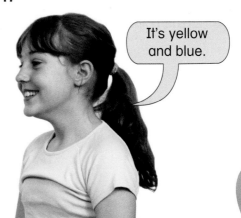
It's yellow and blue.

Step 2 – Practise

1 **Circle the correct words.**

1 The helicopter is flying **below /** **near** the island.

2 The boy is **behind / next to** the man.

3 The woman is **opposite / behind** the man.

4 The helicopter is **next to / above** the boat now.

5 The boat is **next to / below** the helicopter.

6 The girl is **next to / opposite** the woman.

2 **Listen and colour.** 18

Remember! Listen carefully.
Don't colour everything!

3 **Look at the picture in exercise 1. Listen and write.** 19

Step 3 – Pass!

1 Listen and colour and write. There is one example. 20

Step 1 – Prepare

1 **Look and write the words.**

1 ......nurse......

2 ....

3 ....

4 ....

5 ....

6 ....

7 ....

pirate
teacher
doctor
~~nurse~~
clown
driver
farmer

2 **Look and write the words.**

1 A nurse works ......in a hospital...... .

2 A clown works ....

3 A farmer works ....

4 A pirate lives ....

5 A bus driver works ....

6 A teacher works ....

at a children's party
in a school
~~in a hospital~~
in a bus
on a farm
on an island

3 **Look and write the words.**

1 Lions and parrots live here. ......the jungle......

2 A pet mouse lives here. ....

3 A pet fish lives in this. ....

4 Goats like to walk to the top of this. ....

5 A shark and a whale live here. ....

6 A duck swims here. ....

a bowl
~~the jungle~~
a lake
a mountain
the sea
a cage

4 Look and write the words.

aunt   cousin   mum
grandfather   ~~grandmother~~
dad   sister   uncle

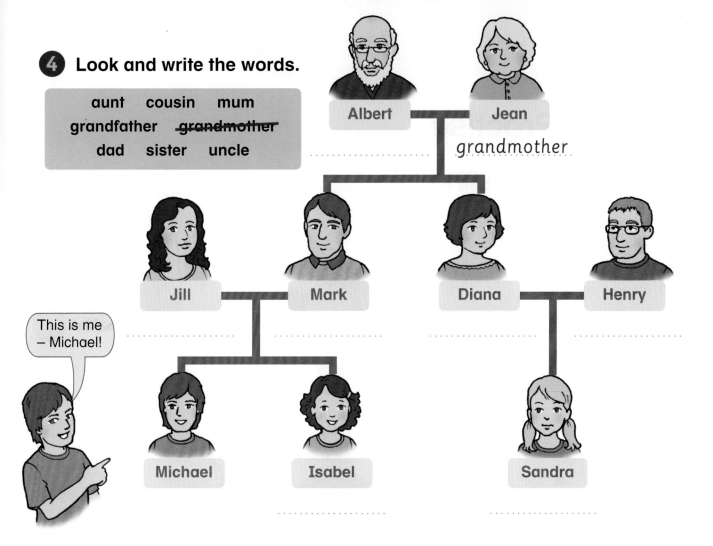

This is me – Michael!

grandmother

5 Look at the picture in exercise 4. Write *T* (true) or *F* (false).

1 Jean and Albert are my grandparents.   T
2 My parents are Diana and Henry.   ....
3 My father is Jean and Albert's son.   ....
4 Jill is Jean and Albert's daughter.   ....
5 Sandra is Albert's granddaughter.   ....
6 Henry is my uncle.   ....

6 Write words from exercise 1 to 5.

family	jobs	places
son	doctor	mountain

25

Step 2 – Practise

1 **Match the words and the pictures.**

1	clown	e
2	parrot	
3	doctor and nurse	
4	panda	
5	rabbit	
6	driver	

a

b

c

d

e

f

2 **Write the words.**

1 He wears funny clothes and he's got a big red nose. *a clown*

2 It lives in a cage and it's got long ears. ....

3 It lives in the jungle. It's black and white. ....

4 It lives on an island, in a tree. It's red, green and blue. ....

5 He drives a lorry or a bus. ....

6 They work in a hospital. ....

Step 3 – Pass!

1 **Look and read. Choose the correct words and write them on the lines.**

parents

grandparents

an aunt

a forest

an island

a parrot

a pirate

a panda

1 It's in the middle of the sea. .... *an island* ......

2 They're my mother and father. ....

3 She's my mother's sister. ....

4 They're my parents' mother and father. ....

5 It lives in a tree in the jungle. ....

6 There are lots of trees here. ....

Step 1 – Prepare

1 **Look and write the words.**

balcony   basement   downstairs   fan   ~~upstairs~~   lift   shower

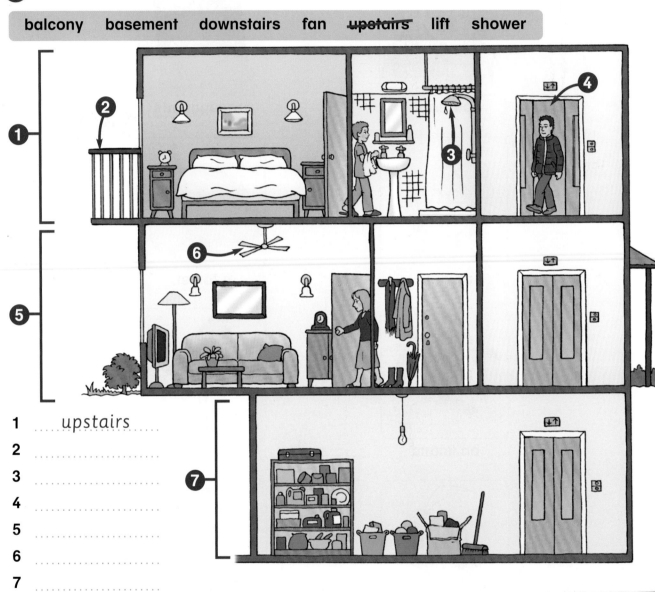

1 ....upstairs....
2 ....
3 ....
4 ....
5 ....
6 ....
7 ....

2 **Look at the picture again. Write *T* (true) or *F* (false).**

upstairs ⬆
downstairs ⬇

1 The house has got two floors.   F
2 There isn't a girl on the balcony.   ....
3 The bedroom is downstairs.   ....
4 The boy has got a towel and a toothbrush.   ....
5 A man is coming out of the lift.   ....
6 The balcony is on the ground floor.   ....

Remember!

3 Circle the odd word out.

1 laugh   cry   (rain)
2 shower   upstairs   bathroom
3 balcony   towel   basement
4 fan   wash   cook
5 toothbrush   towel   puppy
6 film   teeth   video

4 Look at the letters. Write the words.

1 Jill is **aglgiunh** laughing at a TV film.
2 Tony is **nshagwi** .... his face.
3 Dad is **algntnip** .... flowers in the garden.
4 Sue is **gryaircn** .... a big box.
5 Mum is **kgnocio** .... lunch in the kitchen.
6 Ann is **menidgra** .... about a new puppy!

5 Ask and answer.

What is Jill laughing at?

A TV film.

Remember!

dream **about**

laugh **at**

29

Step 2 – Practise

1 **Look and draw a line to match the sentence halves.**

1	A boy	is carrying a puppy.
2	Two children	is cooking.
3	A woman	are in the lift.
4	Two people	is dreaming about dinner.
5	A cat	are laughing.
6	A girl	is washing his face.

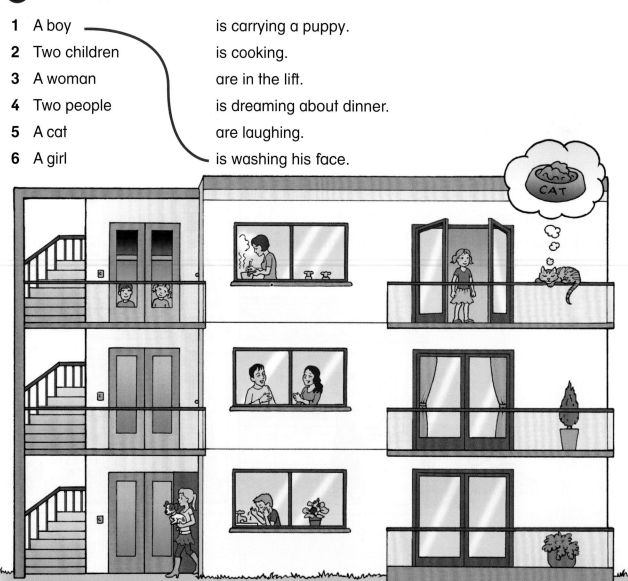

2 **Look and write *yes* or *no*.**

1 A girl is coming out of the flat on the ground floor.   ...yes...

2 The person in the ground floor flat is cooking.   ....

3 The woman in the second floor flat upstairs is laughing.   ....

4 There's a balcony on the first floor.   ....

5 A girl is standing on the balcony.   ....

6 The cat is playing.   ....

Remember! Look carefully at all the words!

Step 3 – Pass!

1 Look and read. Write *yes* or *no*.

1 A woman is carrying flowers. .....no....

2 There are three floors in this house. ....

3 A girl is laughing at the puppy. ....

4 The puppy has got a blanket. ....

5 A man is coming out of the basement. ....

6 Grandpa is dreaming about the sea. ....

Reading & Writing PART **3**

Step 1 – Prepare

1 Find and write five words.

a	n	h	l	e	t	e	a	t	h	s
h	e	a	d	a	c	h	e	t	v	c
c	d	c	o	m	e	m	a	i	l	o
t	o	o	t	h	a	c	h	e	w	u
c	p	l	e	a	r	e	l	d	o	g
d	l	d	o	o	a	r	m	s	e	h
s	t	o	m	a	c	h	a	c	h	e
f	o	o	t	b	h	a	i	r	e	r
w	s	i	t	e	e	a	r	r	i	s

a ......cold......   b ....

c ....   d ....   e ....   f ....

2 Look and match to the pictures in exercise 1.

1 I've got a cough. ....

2 I've got earache. ....

3 I've got a cold. ....a....

4 I've got toothache. ....

5 I've got stomach ache. ....

6 I've got a headache. ....

3 What does the doctor say? Circle the correct words.

Remember!

1 You **must** / mustn't drink lots of water.

2 You **must** / **mustn't** listen to loud music.

3 You **must** / **mustn't** play outside.

4 You **must** / **mustn't** eat any sweets.

5 You **must** / **mustn't** stay in bed.

6 You **must** / **mustn't** go to school.

must = **DO** it!
mustn't = **DON'T** do it!

4 Write *T* (true) or *F* (false).

1 Robert's fine. Nothing's the matter with him.   F

2 He's in the hospital.   ....

3 He's hurt his leg.   ....

4 He's got a temperature.   ....

5 A doctor is with him.   ....

6 A nurse is there.   ....

Remember!

He's = He **is**

He's = He **has**

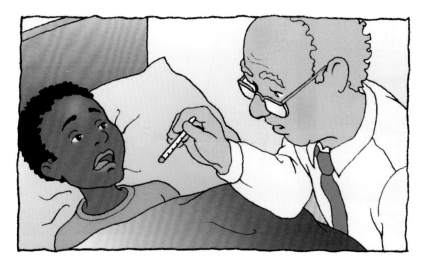

5 Draw a line to match the questions and answers.

1 What's the matter?   Yes, I am.

2 Does your head hurt?   I've got a cough.

3 Can you walk?   Yes, I have.

4 Are you hot?   Yes, please.

5 Have you got a temperature?   Yes, I can.

6 Would you like a drink?   Yes, it does.

Remember! Read everything, then choose the right answer!

6 Circle the correct words.

1 Can you open your eyes? Yes, I **am /(can)/ do**.

2 Is your head hot? Yes, **I am / it is / it does**.

3 Does your throat hurt? No, **it doesn't / I can't / it isn't**.

4 Have you got a headache? Yes, I **have / do / can**.

5 Do you like reading? Yes, I **am / do / can**.

6 Is this your book? No, **I don't / it is / it isn't**.

Reading & Writing PART 3

Step 2 – Practise

1 **Look and write the words.**

head ~~home~~ better comic mother temperature

1 The boy is in bed at ..... home .....

2 His .... is with him.

3 She is taking his ....

4 His .... hurts.

5 Later, he starts to feel ....

6 Now he wants to read a ....

Remember!
Draw clear circles.

2 **Circle the correct words.**

1 Where does it hurt?
   A In my head.
   B When I sit up.
   C Because I'm ill.

2 Did you play in the rain yesterday?
   A No, it isn't raining.
   B Yes, it was.
   C Yes, we did.

3 Can you talk?
   A No, I don't.
   B Yes, please.
   C Yes, but it hurts.

4 Would you like a nice warm drink?
   A No, I'm not warm.
   B Yes, please.
   C Yes, it's warm in here.

Step 3 – Pass!

1 **Read the text and choose the best answer.**

1 **Miss Jones:** What's the matter, Lucy?

  Lucy: **A** My neck hurts!

  B Yes, please.

  C No, it doesn't.

2 **Miss Jones:** Did you fall off your bike?

  Lucy: **A** No, it wasn't.

  B Yes, I did.

  C No, thanks.

3 **Miss Jones:** Have you got a headache?

  Lucy: **A** No, it isn't.

  B No, I don't.

  C Yes, I have.

4 **Miss Jones:** Can you hold a pencil?

  Lucy: **A** Yes, it's not good.

  B No, I can't.

  C No, I don't like it.

5 **Lucy:** I can't write the test, Miss Jones.

  Miss Jones: **A** Yes, you write it.

  B Yes, you do.

  C No, you can't write it, but you can tell me the answers!

Reading & Writing PART 4

Step 1 – Prepare

1 **Look and write the animal words.**

 **1** It's a b <u>a t</u> .

 **4** This is a l _ _ n.

 **2** It's a k _ n _ a _ o _ .

 **5** They're s _ a _ k _ .

 **3** That's a p _ n _ a .

 **6** They're d _ l _ h _ n _ .

2 **Ask and answer.**

Remember!

What are these?

What's this?

They're dolphins.

It's a ...

| Singular | this is / it's |
| Plural | these are / they're |

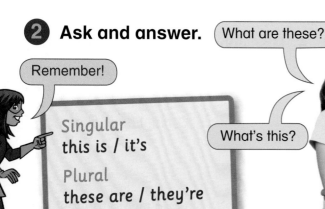

3 **Look and write the animal words.**

1 It's black and white and it lives in the jungle. ....*panda*....

2 They're grey. They like swimming. They like playing with people. ....

3 It's brown. It likes jumping. ....

4 It's smaller than a parrot. It's brown. It can fly. ....

5 It's brown. It's a big cat. It lives in the jungle. ....

6 They're grey, with big, strong teeth. Don't swim near them! ....

4 Look and write the animal words.

a lehaw .... *whale* ....

b tibbar ....

c tentik ....

d pypup ....

e rabe ....

f rotpar ....

5 Circle the correct words.

1 A parrot sits in a (cage) / farm.

2 A whale is **big / heavier** than a fly.

3 My cat is playing with her three **kittens / ears**.

4 A rabbit can jump. Its **nose / ears** are longer than its legs.

5 My dog has got two brown **puppies / dog**.

6 Look! There's a crocodile! I'm **bear / afraid**.

Remember! Think about the whole sentence!

6 Write words from exercise 4 and 5.

animals and birds	colours	parts of the body	places	actions
parrot				

37

Reading & Writing PART 4

Remember!
Circle **two** words!

Step 2 – Practise

1 Circle <u>two</u> correct words.

1 What can you eat?   ~~bananas~~ / ~~coconuts~~ / tigers
2 What animals live in the jungle?   lions / sharks / monkeys
3 What do you find in trees?   fish / coconuts / parrots
4 What is red and blue?   a fish / a banana / a parrot
5 What can you play with?   leaves / a ball / a toy
6 Which are smaller than a panda?   a coconut / a whale / a bat

2 Circle the correct words.

Remember! Read
the whole sentence!

The jungle is a very interesting place. Lots of animals and birds live
there. Look at the **1** panda / parrot. It's red and blue. It isn't flying.
It's sitting in a **2** leaves / tree. Some monkeys are climbing the tree.
They're climbing higher and higher! They're **3** eating / playing with
bananas! **4** Tigers / Sharks live in the jungle, too. I can see one
hiding in the forest. A **5** bear / panda is sitting under a tree.
A **6** lion / coconut is going to fall on its head!

Step 3 – Pass!

1 **Read the story. Choose a word from the box.**
Write the correct word next to numbers 1 – 6.

brother	**sister**
parrot	**dolphin**
tree	**camera**
sea	**clouds**

My favourite story is about a brother and **1** ......*sister*...... .
One day, they went for a walk by the **2** .... The girl
stopped and took out her camera. She wanted to take a photo of
some **3** .... They were swimming and playing in the
water. The boy walked into the forest. He saw a **4** ....
in a **5** .... He called his sister. 'Mary! Where are you?'
The parrot flew up into the clouds. It flew to the sea. Mary heard it say,
'Mary! Where are you?' She followed the parrot. It took her nearer to
the forest, and then she found her **6** .... again!

Reading & Writing PART 5

Step 1 – Prepare

1 Look and draw a line to match the words and pictures.

hungry

naughty

thirsty

wet

surprised

tired

2 Find and write six words. Then write their opposites.

rightatstrongnoeasybexcitingmalstraighthot

1   right   wrong   4

2   5

3   6

3 Look and draw a line to match the sentence halves.

 Jack    Amy    Peter    Sally 

1 The children had a test   because he was hot.

2 Jack couldn't do the test   when they went to school on Monday.

3 Amy thought the test was easy   because she knew the answers.

4 Peter wasn't happy   because he was tired.

5 Sally stopped writing   when she finished the test.

4 **Circle the correct words.**

Yesterday the children **1** (wrote a test)/ played a game
when they went to school. Jack couldn't do the test. It was
2 **difficult / easy** for him because he was very tired. His
answers were **3** **right / wrong**. Amy **4** **knew / didn't know**
the answers because she always works hard. Peter didn't feel
well because he was **5** **hot and thirsty / cold and weak**. Sally
finished the test because she thought it was **6** **boring / easy**.

5 **Write the answers. Write three words.**

Remember!
Count the words!

| ~~claseroom~~ | did | didn't | early | ~~in~~ | it |
| Monday | no | ~~the~~ | they | was | yes |

1 Where were the children? .... in .... the ...... classroom
2 Did they use their books? ....
3 What day was it? ....
4 Was it early or late? ....
5 Did they all wear blue sweaters? ....
6 Did it rain? ....

6 **Ask and answer.**

Where were
the children?

In the
classroom.

Step 2 – Practise

1 **Read the story. Write the answers.**

John woke up. It was a sunny day outside. 'I want to play football!'
he thought. Then he sat up. It was time for school! He got up and got
dressed quickly. He wore his grey trousers and his white shirt. He ran
to school. 'I mustn't be late!' he thought. When he arrived, he was hot,
tired and thirsty. Where were all the children? They were at home – it
was Saturday! There was no school!

> at home   ~~go to school~~   he didn't want
> his clothes   at school   on Saturday

John couldn't play football because he had to **1** .....go to school......
He put on **2** .... – a white shirt and some grey
trousers. He ran to school because **3** .... to be late.
But the other children weren't **4** .... They were
5 .... 'I was wrong! It isn't a school day!' thought
John. 'We don't go to school **6** ....!'

2 **Count the words in your answers. How many words?**

1 ....3.......   4 ....
2 ....   5 ....
3 ....   6 ....

Step 3 – Pass!

1 Look at the picture and read the story. Write some words to complete the sentences. You can use 1, 2 or 3 words.

It was Susie's birthday, and she woke up early. 'It's an exciting day!' she thought. She ran downstairs quickly because she wanted to see her presents! But her parents and brother weren't in the living room. The house was quiet. 'Where are they? Perhaps they're in the garden!' she thought. She went outside but she didn't see them. Susie was sad. She walked slowly back to the house. She opened the kitchen door – and they all jumped out! Her parents and brother were hiding behind the furniture! They had presents. And in the hall, there was a new red bike!

Remember!
Write 1, 2 or 3
words only.

1 Susie woke up early because it _was her birthday_ that day.

2 She was excited because she wanted .... her presents!

3 Her parents and her brother .... the living room when she went downstairs.

4 She couldn't see them ....

5 When she opened the .... door, they all jumped out!

6 Her birthday present was a ....

43

Reading & Writing PART 6

Step 1 – Prepare

1 **Write the answers.**

1 31 + 24 = *fifty-five*	22
2 37 + 7 = ...	89
3 eighty + nine = ...	**fifty-eight**
4 40 + 18 = ...	~~**fifty-five**~~
5 seventeen + five = ...	**forty-four**
6 21 + 46 = ...	**sixty-seven**

2 **Look and draw a line to match the numbers.**

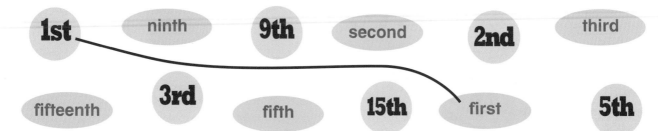

1st — ninth — 9th — second — 2nd — third

fifteenth — 3rd — fifth — 15th — first — 5th

3 **Look and write.**

Our birthdays are all in the same month. Mine is on the ❶ .... *twentieth* ....., and Fred's is on the ❷ .... Vicky's is on the ❸ ...., and John's is on the ❹ .... Peter's is on the ❺ .... day of the month, and Sally's is on the ❻ ....

4 Read and circle the picture.

1 Circle the third cloud.

4 Circle the fifth rainbow.

2 Circle the fourth star.

5 Circle the second moon.

3 Circle the first sun.

6 Circle the sixth island.

5 Circle the correct words.

1 How many colours **have /(has)/ had** a rainbow got?

2 After it rains, what **must / will / does** you see in the clouds?

3 How **much / old / many** stars come out at night?

4 Is the Sun **big / bigger / biggest** than the Moon?

5 **Do / Were / Are** people live on the Moon?

6 **Do / Would / Are** you like to go to the Moon one day?

6 Read the answers to the questions in exercise 5. Ask and answer.

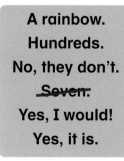

A rainbow.
Hundreds.
No, they don't.
~~Seven.~~
Yes, I would!
Yes, it is.

Step 2 – Practise

1 Draw a line to match the sentence halves.

Remember! Is the sentence about ... yesterday? today? tomorrow?

1 Tomorrow it	I went to the cinema.
2 Last weekend	play table tennis.
3 On Mondays my mother always	am reading a comic.
4 Next Saturday Fred	is playing football.
5 Every Tuesday I	will be my birthday.
6 Today I	goes shopping.

2 Circle the correct words.

1 There are hundreds of **stars** / **moons** / **sea** in the world.

2 I like **watch** / **draw** / **dreaming** about the Moon at night.

3 Look! It's getting dark, and I can see the first **star** / **sunny** / **sea**.

4 My grandma is an **seventy-eight** / **help** / **old** woman.

5 It's very **windy** / **raining** / **temperature** today.

6 I'm reading a book about the world. It's **like** / **exciting** / **treasure**.

3 Look and write the words.

I love **1** ....swimming.... in the sea. So, yesterday

we **2** .... by car to the beach. It was

a **3** .... day. 'Let's **4** ....

into the water!' I said. Then it **5** .... to rain!

My mum and dad **6** .... to the car.

But my brother and I laughed. 'We want to get wet!' we said.

We took off our clothes and went swimming!

go
ran
started
sunny
~~swimming~~
went

Step 3 – Pass!

1 Read the text. Choose the right words and write them on the lines.

When you **1** .... _look_ .... at the Sun and the Moon, which looks bigger?
What do you think? Here is the answer. The Sun is 400 times **2** ....
than the Moon! It looks small, **3** .... it is very far away.

The Sun is very big, but did you know, it is smaller than all the stars?

We can see the Moon very **4** ...., because the Sun shines on it. The
Sun shines on us, too. That's why we are warm **5** .... it is light.

The Moon goes round and round us. It takes about 27 days to go round us. More than
forty years ago, the first man **6** .... on the Moon. There is no wind
on the Moon and no weather. So you can still see where the man walked!

1 (look)	looked	looking
2 big	bigger	biggest
3 where	who	because
4 good	quiet	well
5 and	but	that
6 walks	is walking	walked

47

Speaking

Step 1 – Prepare

1 Write the words in the best place.

balcony   basement   dolphin   tiger
island   lift   panda   parrot   shark

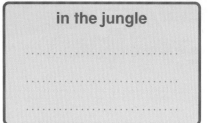
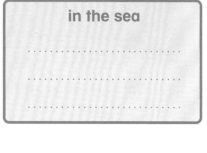

in the jungle	in a house	in the sea
....	................balcony............	....
....	....	....
....	....	....

2 Ask and answer.

Do you find a balcony in the sea?

No, you don't. You find it in a house.

3 Read and tick ✔ the correct words.

1 It's got two legs.	✔ monkey	shark	dolphin
2 It's part of a house.	panda	basement	hospital
3 It can't swim.	parrot	dolphin	shark
4 There are books here.	lift	library	balcony
5 It can go up and down.	balcony	mountain	lift
6 There are trees here.	lift	basement	island

4 Write the words.

a milk
b ....
c ....
d ....
e ....
f ....

5 Listen and number the pictures in the correct order. 🎧 21

a ☐

b ☐

c ☐

d 1

6 Ask and answer.

Why didn't Paul want breakfast?

Because he wasn't hungry.

49

Speaking

Step 2 – Practise

1 Look at the pictures. Write A or B.

1 The parrot is talking. **B**

2 There are two children. ☐

3 The panda isn't eating leaves. ☐

4 A crocodile is swimming. ☐

5 A frog is jumping into the water. ☐

6 There is one grey animal. ☐

2 Talk to your partner. Find the differences.

 In picture A the panda is eating.

 In picture B the panda is sleeping.

3 Read and tick ✔ the correct words.

1 There aren't any animals in this place. ☐ zoo   ✔ hospital   ☐ island

2 They eat leaves. ☐ doctors   ☐ boys   ☐ pandas

3 It lives in water and it hasn't got feet. ☐ a fish   ☐ an elephant   ☐ a parrot

4 They've got two legs. ☐ elephants   ☐ lions   ☐ children

5 You can sit on it. ☐ a chair   ☐ a lift   ☐ a race

6 It's big. It doesn't sit in a tree. ☐ a parrot   ☐ an elephant   ☐ a monkey

4 Match the pictures and the sentences.

1 | c ○

2 | ☐ ○

3 | ☐

4 | ☐

a 'We want to go for a swim!' they said. They ran to the sea.

b No, it wasn't a shark. It was a dolphin!

c The family was on an island. They looked at the sea from the balcony.

d There was something in the sea. Was it a shark?

Speaking

Step 3 – Pass!

1 Spot the difference.

2 Picture story.

3 Odd-one-out.

1

2

3

4

Listening

Part 1 (5 questions)

Listen and draw lines. There is one example. 22

Peter	Paul	Mary	Jane

the teacher	Fred	Sally

Listening

Part 2 (5 questions)

Listen and write. There is one example. 23

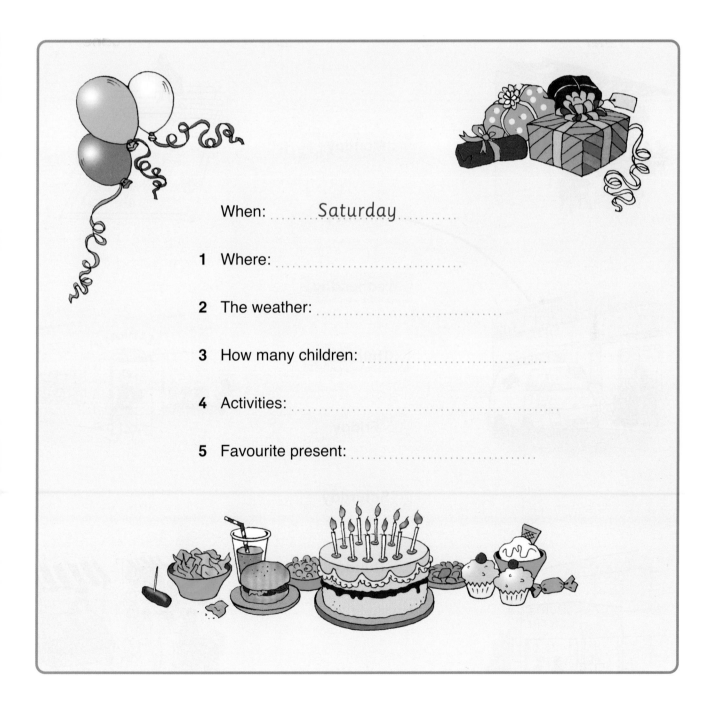

When: .... Saturday ....

1 Where: ....

2 The weather: ....

3 How many children: ....

4 Activities: ....

5 Favourite present: ....

Listening

Part 3 (5 questions)

What did Mary do last week? 🎧 24
Listen and draw a line from the day to the correct picture.
There is one example.

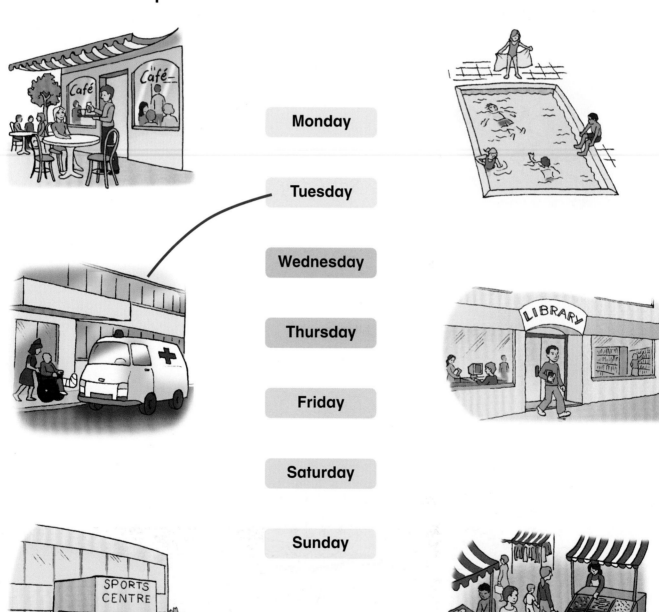

Monday

Tuesday

Wednesday

Thursday

Friday

Saturday

Sunday

Listening

Part 4 (5 questions)

Listen and tick ✔ the box. There is one example. 25

What did the children do yesterday?

A ☐

B ✔

C ☐

1 What did they take?

A ☐

B ☐

C ☐

2 What was the weather like?

A ☐

B ☐

C ☐

3 What did they find?

A

B

C

4 What was in the tree?

A

B

C

5 What did they do at home?

A

B

C

Listening

Part 5 (5 questions)

Listen and colour and write. There is one example. 26

Reading & Writing

Part 1 (6 questions)

Look and read. Choose the correct words and write them on the lines.

nurse

toothbrush

homework

aunt

glass

towel

clown

teeth

PRACTICE TEST

Example

You do this when you come home from school.   homework

Questions

1   You use this after you eat, to clean your teeth.   ....

2   He's got a funny face, and a big, red nose.   ....

3   You drink milk, water or orange juice in this.   ....

4   She takes your temperature when you don't feel well.   ....

5   You use this after you have a swim or a shower.   ....

6   This is your mother or father's sister.   ....

Reading & Writing

Part 2 (6 questions)

Look and read. Write *yes* or *no*.

Examples

There are three children.   ...yes...

There is a whale in the sea.   ....no....

PRACTICE TEST

Questions

1   There are two fish.   . . . .

2   The crocodile's mouth is open.   . . . .

3   The children aren't afraid.   . . . .

4   Two children are wearing shorts.   . . . .

5   There is some treasure on the beach.   . . . .

6   It's a cold and windy day.   . . . .

Reading & Writing

Part 3 (6 questions)

Read the text and choose the best answer.
Ann's grandmother is talking to her.

Example

Grandma: What are you doing, Ann?

Ann: (**A**) I'm playing a game.

 B I watch a DVD.

 C It's a computer.

Questions

1 Grandma: Why are you happy?

 Ann: **A** Because I won the game!

 B Yes, I won the game.

 C Yes, I am!

PRACTICE TEST

2 Ann: Did you play computer games when you were young?

Grandma: **A** No, I haven't.

B No, I don't.

C No, I didn't.

3 Grandma: Do you like writing emails?

Ann: **A** Yes, I can.

B Yes, I do.

C No, sorry, I can't. I'm busy.

4 Ann: Did you watch TV when you were young?

Grandma: **A** Yes, we did.

B Sorry, I don't know.

C Yes, OK. I'd like to!

5 Grandma: Did your teacher give you any homework today?

Ann: **A** No, they don't.

B Yes, I did.

C Yes, she did.

6 Grandma: Would you like a drink?

Ann: **A** No, I don't.

B Yes, please.

C Yes, I like orange juice.

Reading & Writing

Part 4 (7 questions)

Read the story. Choose a word from the box. Write the correct word next to the numbers 1 – 6. There is one example.

My favourite story is about a brother and sister. Their names were Vicky and Peter. One day, Peter said, 'Shall we go fishing?' 'OK!' said Vicky. 'We can cook the fish for our lunch!'

They went to the _____ lake _____. The water was blue and cold. They

1 _____ in their boat for a long time. Peter said, 'I've caught

something! It's heavy!' But it wasn't a fish. It was a big **2** _____.

'Oh, no!' said Vicky. 'We didn't catch a fish for our lunch. Now we haven't got

anything to eat!' 'Let's sail to that **3** _____ over there,' said Peter.

'I think there's some **4** _____ on the trees.' 'Good idea, I'm hungry,'

said Vicky. When they got there, they found a big, brown bag under the tree. Inside

the bag, there were drinks and **5** _____! And there was a letter.

'Have a nice **6** _____!' they read. 'From Mum and Dad!' The

children laughed. 'What a great idea!' they said.

PRACTICE TEST

Example

lake   sandwiches   box

island   picnic   sailed

swimming   fruit   leaves

7 Choose the best name for the story. Tick ✔ one box.

A story I liked. ☐

Vicky and Peter's favourite story. ☐

My brother and sister's picnic. ☐

Reading & Writing

Part 5 (10 questions)

Look at the pictures and read the story. Write some words to complete the sentences about the story. You can use 1, 2 or 3 words.

Bob plays football

Every day after school, Bob plays football. He's very good at football. He can kick the ball very well! But last Friday, something happened to Bob. He hurt his back. His friend, Fred, said, 'What's the matter, Bob?' Bob said, 'I've hurt myself. I must go and see the doctor. I can't play football now.' Fred helped Bob. They walked to the school doctor.

Examples

Bob likes to ... *play football* ... after school.

He is ..... *good at* ..... kicking the ball.

Questions

1 Bob hurt himself on .... after school.

2 He didn't hurt his foot – he ....

3 Bob has got a .... called Fred. Fred helped him.

The doctor looked at Bob's back. 'Your back is fine,' he said.

The nurse said, 'Have you got a headache?'

'Yes, I have,' said Bob.

'I must take your temperature,' said the nurse. But Bob's temperature wasn't high.

'Now my leg hurts!' said Bob. 'I must sit down.'

4 The doctor didn't find anything wrong with ....

5 The .... Bob's temperature.

6 Bob had to .... because his leg hurt.

Bob sat down. 'Let me look at your leg,' said the doctor. 'Did you fall?'

'No, said Bob. 'I kicked the ball, but I didn't hurt my leg.'

The doctor put his hand on Bob's sock. 'What's this?' he asked.
'You've got something in your sock!' The doctor took out a banana!

Bob said, 'Oh, yes, that's for my lunch! I didn't know where to put it,
you see!'

7 The doctor .... to look at Bob's leg.

8 Bob .... his leg when he kicked the ball.

9 The doctor saw .... in Bob's sock.

10 It was .... ! Bob had his lunch in his sock!

Reading & Writing

Part 6 (5 questions)

Read the text. Choose the right words and write them on the lines.

Bill's party

Example	It .... *was* .... Bill's birthday yesterday!	

1 He .... ten years old.

2 He .... a birthday party and

he got lots of birthday presents. All of Bill's

friends came to his party. His favourite

present was a new CD player. His parents

bought it for him. Bill loves music.

3 He .... lots of CDs. It was

4 a good party. They .... pizza

and sandwiches and they drank lemonade

and orange juice. Then they listened to music

5 and danced, and then they ....

games.

PRACTICE TEST

Example	is	(was)	are
1	does	are	is
2	had	has	is having
3	have	got	gets
4	eat	ate	take
5	played	playing	play

Speaking
Summary of Procedures

The usher introduces the child to the examiner. The examiner asks how old the child is.

1 The examiner asks the child to describe several difference between the two Find the Differences pictures, e.g. 'This is a man but this is a woman.'

2 The examiner tells the child the name of the story and describes the first picture, e.g. 'The girl is running in a race but she falls over. She hurts her leg. I think she's very sad.' The examiner then asks the child to continue telling the story.

3 The examiner demonstrates how to do this task with the first set of our odd-one-out pictures and then asks the child to choose one picture in the other three sets and say which is different and why. For example, 'These are things you do every day, but this is a football.'

4 The examiner asks questions about the child, e.g. 'Who's the youngest in your family?'

Speaking

PRACTICE TEST

Speaking

Practise and Pass

Young Learners English Test

MOVERS

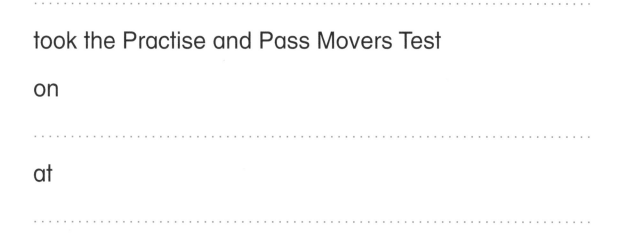

....

took the Practise and Pass Movers Test

on

....

at

....

Listening ☆☆☆☆☆

Reading & Writing ☆☆☆☆☆

Speaking ☆☆☆☆☆

Signed

....